"Sr. Trudy's book is a good guide for involving the entire class in acting out Gospel stories. The questions it provides help students identify with the characters' feelings and to practice their actions, facial expressions, and gestures. This preparation insures that children will not only produce finer plays, but also develop a deeper understanding of Gospel events. The format used for all fifteen plays can serve as a model for catechists to produce additional plays in the future. A bonus of the book is a number of simple patterns for masks and props."

Sr. Kathleen Glavich, SND
Author of *Gospel Plays for Students* and
Acting Out the Miracles and Parables

"Trudy Schommer has written a book that will help teachers and catechists add interest and life to their lessons. In her introduction she says, '...children delight in being able to perform before friends, family, or their classmates.' My own experience says this is as true of seventh to tenth graders as of younger children.

"Trudy Schommer offers very practical and helpful ways to get children 'into' Bible stories in catechetical settings. She gives clear directions for acting out Gospel stories. For each play she lists characters, setting, costume ideas, and movement and dialogue exercises. *Easiest Gospel Plays Ever* certainly makes Gospel dramatizations easy for catechists—even inexperienced ones!"

Barbara Gargiulo
Catechist and teacher,
Plano, Texas

"Busy catechists will welcome this excellent tool for enticing students to enter wholeheartedly into Gospel stories. Without the burden of memorizing scripts or building extensive sets or costumes, Schommer suggests step-by-step directions for dramatizing the teachings of Jesus. She shows catechists how to use a questioning technique to help students decide how the characters feel, how they move, what their facial expressions should be. By gently guiding students to 'walk in the character's shoes,' she enables them to 'own' the stories and to broaden their understanding of Gospel messages. Because of the complete and easy-to-follow directions (Schommer seems to have thought of everything), even the novice catechist or those who have never attempted dramatizations before will be successful at using this exciting and technique!"

Carole MacClennan
Author of *When Jesus Was Young* and
Learning By Doing: 150 Activities to Enrich Religion Classes for Young Children

"I have always been one of those people who 'skips over' dramatizations. They were just not my thing. *Easiest Gospel Plays Ever* has converted me.

"Schommer's plays engage students in Gospel stories in ways that truly touch their faith lives. To live the story, to come to know Jesus and the other characters intimately through the exploration of their feelings and actions, is the way all of us need to be in touch with Scripture. What a wonderful way to 'do' the Gospels!"

Karen Leslie, Director of Religious Education
Author of *Faith and Little Children*

"What an innovative and wonderful way to bring the Gospel to life! Trudy Schommer has not only simplified Gospel plays for both the novice and veteran teacher, she also offers a way to tap into the tremendous imaginations of children. By encouraging children to actually live through the actions and emotions of biblical characters, *Easiest Gospel Plays Ever* has the potential of opening their hearts and minds in a powerful and permanent way."

Deborah Roslak
Author of *Dear Jesus, Dear Child*

"I especially liked the 15 Bible stories that Trudy Schommer chose to dramatize because they are probably familiar to most children. Although she doesn't mention the word 'mime,' I can see that it, too, has a place in these stories. Or, a teacher may also choose to add to or change the dialogue, and that's okay, too. This is quite a unique book!"

Nancy J. Reece
Author of *Celebrations of the Word for Children*

Easiest GOSPEL PLAYS EVER

Trudy Schommer

TWENTY-THIRD PUBLICATIONS

Mystic, Connecticut 06355

Twenty-Third Publications
185 Willow Street
P.O. Box 180
Mystic CT 06355
(203) 536-2611
800-321-0411

ISBN 0-89622-550-X

Contents

Easiest Gospel Plays Ever

Introduction

Most children delight in being able to "put on a different hat" and perform before friends, family, or their classmates. Performing is also a wonderful learning tool. Some of my most delightful and remembered experiences were my elementary education days when we were allowed to perform in a drama of some kind.

In order to really "act out" a part, it is necessary that the actors and actresses get into the feelings of the person whose part they are taking. This is especially important when we are dealing with stories from sacred Scripture.

Having been a teacher for many years and a Director of Religious Education in several parishes, I have been responsible for helping volunteer catechists. Many of these volunteers were not trained teachers and all too often the teacher's manual would simply instruct them: "Dramatize this story with your students." Without any specific help given, most of them would skip over the suggestion. They were afraid to dramatize, not really knowing where to begin.

And so I began writing out lesson plans for catechists to use in their classes, based solely on the Scripture stories their lessons covered. Before long, *Easiest Gospel Plays Ever* was conceived and born.

Walking in the Character's Shoes

In order to "walk in the shoes of the character," it is necessary to get in touch with the character's *feelings*. This is not always easy. Questions need to be asked, and we need to probe a little to get in touch with their feelings as well as our own. To facilitate this, I have studied some of the more familiar stories from the gospels and put together some questions to guide teachers. This helps the students get into the shoes of the character before they begin the actual dramatization.

The Easy Way to Dramatize

The method employed in this book is the easy way to dramatize; it requires little planning beyond the steps provided. Since the rehearsal is done by the entire class and costumes are kept to a minimum, there is also much less frustration for the teacher and the students. This method increases the children's comprehension skills, their ability to follow directions, and enhances their own self-esteem. They also learn to work together as a group.

Involving the Entire Class

Before being concerned about what to say, your students will get in touch with the feelings of the characters, practice facial expressions, and move like the characters. These exercises are done by the entire class so everyone learns about each character. By practicing together how to throw out a fish net, feel the joy of being cured, experience sight for the first time, or feel the joy of returning home to a forgiving father, children will be able to express the emotions of the story characters.

No Script?

Your students will not have to carry a script around with them during the dramatization. They are not tied to memorized lines. They can simply focus on the sequence of the story and the feelings of the characters, and how the characters would naturally respond to those feelings. They will have heard the story several times, will have gone through the actions, and will have had discussions of the entire story. They can thus respond in appropriate ways.

No Costumes?

The costumes used in traditional Christmas pageants can be used: pieces of material, cloth ribbons or belts, old dresses, etc. For the most part, however, even these are unnecessary, although they are helpful. Go with what you have, and over the years you can quickly build up a supply of costumes from garage sales and second-hand stores. Often the apparel can be obtained very reasonably if you tell the merchant why you want them.

When to Use These Dramas

The Contents page indicates when in the liturgical year the Scripture stories in this volume are read at Mass. You should feel free to use these plays not only shortly before the Sunday the Scripture is proclaimed, but on other occasions during the school year, as well. You may enhance a lesson plan, on reconciliation, for example, by using the Prodigal Son drama, or a lesson on love of neighbors by enacting the Good Samaritan play. Near Thanksgiving Day, the students might find the Ten Lepers or the Bartimaeus drama inspiring. When treating the Eucharist in class, consider using the Multiplication of the Loaves and Fishes. When vocation is a topic for class consideration, use the Call of Peter, Andrew, James, and John. And so on. Your sense of what is appropriate for your students will suggest many occasions to use these dramas.

Using This Book: Step by Step

Familiarize the children with the story. This can be done in many different ways. You can read the story to them. They can read the story. You can tell them the story using stick figures on the chalkboard, using the flannel board, etc.

•Discuss the story with the students. Many times your lesson plan will give you the questions to use.

•Use thought questions to evoke the characters' feelings in the students. Then practice with them in sequence the body responses of the characters, as well as their actions. This is where this book comes in—by providing appropriate questions that lead the children into bodily, facial, and verbal responses.

•List the characters in the play, soliciting them from the students.

•Choose the students for each character. You may want to add characters, or focus on different ones with each performance.

•Give out costumes, if you are using them.

•Set the stage. Decide where each "scene" will take place. If any props are needed (sometimes students can be the props), these can be set up.

•Perform! The narration should be read by the teacher so that pauses are observed in order to allow the necessary dialogue. After experience with this type of dramatization, students may be able to read the narrations.

•Evaluate: What did you like, not like, about how the play went in general? About how the characters played their parts? (To the performers themselves): What would you do differently if you did it again?

•Perhaps go through the play again with a new cast. Evaluate this experience.

Notes

Just a few notes to make it all a little easier. In the guided questions I sometimes speak of a character's body being "open" or "closed." This is a way of asking: Will the character's body be outgoing and vital, or will it be tired and drooped as when one feels exhausted, closed in?

Since many of these stories involve Jesus, it might be helpful to have some distinguishing costume that only Jesus wears each time he is in the story. An example might be just a red strip of cloth that the child would wear over his or her shoulder. Note, too, that Jesus can be played by girls and boys. We are all "other Christs"!

In some of the stories, if you want a character to be really clear about saying a certain line from the dialogue, you may type up ahead of time a note card for the child with just the desired lines on it. This is not necessary, however, and a little prompting from the narrator may be just as good.

I have tried to indicate by a carat in parentheses (^) where the players might want to insert additional dialogue in the script. However, the narrator-teacher is the best judge of when this could happen. The lines that are in quotations may be read by the narrator or spoken by the characters.

Above all, the children should enjoy the play! The more you do this type of dramatization with your students, the easier it will become for them and the more they will enjoy it. They will begin to ask to put on more plays!

The Ten Lepers

Luke 17:11-19

One day Jesus was walking toward a small village. Ten people who were sick called out to Jesus. They stood far away from him because they had an ugly skin disease called leprosy.

They begged Jesus to help them. (^) (Remember, this sign means that students may want to add spontaneous dialogue at this point.) Jesus felt sorry for them. He could see that they were very sick. He understood how much they were hurting.

"Go show yourself to the priests," Jesus told them. (^) They did as Jesus had told them to do. On their way to Jerusalem all of them were completely healed. (^)

One of them, a Samaritan, ran his hands over his face and arms. He could feel how smooth they felt. All of the sores were healed! He praised and thanked God. (^)

Then the man went back to find Jesus. (^) When he saw Jesus, he ran over to him and thanked him.

"Were not ten healed?" asked Jesus. "Where are the other nine? Stand up and go. Your faith has saved you."

Movement and Dialogue Exercise

TEN LEPERS—The ten persons were all sick. Some needed walking sticks.
How would they walk? Show me.
Would their bodies be open or closed?
Would their faces show their pain? How?
What would they be saying to Jesus when they saw him?

JESUS—How would Jesus respond to them?
Would he be angry at them?
What would his face look like?

TEN LEPERS—(Before being accepted back into their community, it was the custom to
    be checked by the priests to be sure they were healed of the infectious disease.)
How do you think they felt when Jesus told them to go show themselves to the priests?
Might some doubt? Why or why not?
What would they probably say to each other?
What would they say when they realized they were healed?
How would their bodies change?
Would their bodies now be open or closed?
What would they do with their walking sticks?

ONE LEPER RETURNS—How would his response differ from the others?
What would he say to Jesus when he found him?
How would he respond to what Jesus says to him?

Stage Setting

Jesus can enter from left. The ten lepers can be to the back of the extreme right. The lepers pass behind left while they are cured. The one leper goes back to right to find Jesus. The only props you may want are a few large rag bandages and walking sticks for the lepers. They take off the rags when they are cured.

Characters

Narrator
Jesus
Ten lepers

Dramatization

Now re-read the story and have the students respond in the appropriate ways.

The Unforgiving Servant

Matthew 18:23-30

There was once a servant who owed a king a large sum of money. One day the king called the servant to see him. (^) "You must pay me the money you owe me," the king said.

"Oh, please, I do not have the money," the servant replied.

"Well then you must be sold, your wife, children, and all your property to pay the debt," the king replied.

But the servant begged, "I can't pay you back now, but I promise to pay it all back soon."

The king felt sorry for the poor servant. So he thought for a moment and said, "Well, all right. I forgive your debt. There's no need to worry any more."

The servant was so relieved! But as he was walking home, he met a man who owed him a dollar. The servant grabbed the man. "Pay me back the money you owe me."

The man fell to his knees and begged, "Please give me a little more time. I'm a poor man, but I'll pay you as soon as I can."

The servant got very angry and hit the man. "I want my money now!" he shouted.

"Please, I don't have it right now." But the servant had the man put in jail until he paid the dollar he owed.

Movement and Dialogue Exercise

KING—Practice how a king would walk and stand.

How would a king talk?

When the king is thinking, how might he show this?

SERVANT—If you were to talk to the king, how would you feel?

And if you owed him money, how would you feel?

How would you talk to him?

How would the face of the servant change when he realizes that the king has forgiven him?

How would he feel?

How would he walk home after being forgiven the debt?

Have you ever been forgiven for something you did?

How did you feel?

How would the whole body of the servant (face, shoulders, etc.) change when he saw the man who owed him the dollar? Why?

What is the servant feeling? Superior? Arrogant?

How would he speak to the man who owed him the dollar?

SECOND SERVANT—How would the man who owed the servant a dollar be feeling? How would he show that he was poor and had no money?

Note
There is a lot of dialogue in this story, but most of it can be ad libbed once you have gone over the story and discussed the difference between the response of the king and that of the servant. The narrator's part can be highlighted, leaving out the dialogue; thus she or he will remember to allow for ad libbing.

Stage Setting
The first part with the king can be done on one side of the stage space with the servant moving to the other side for the second half. Decide ahead of time if the king will be pacing as he talks to the servant or if he will be seated. Proceed accordingly.

Costumes and Props
Children love to dress up, so a long gown or train for the king would be great. However, if time is limited, a simple crown for the king from the pattern on page 8 would suffice.

Characters

Narrator
King
Servant
Second servant

Directions for the King's Crown

You will need:
Pattern for crown
Yellow or gold construction paper
Colored pens or crayons (or special colored scraps of paper)
Tagboard 1 1/2" x 24"

1. Duplicate the crown on yellow construction paper.
2. Cut out the crown.
3. Color the jewels with colored pens or cut out colored pieces of paper and glue them on the jewel outlines.
4. Measure a tagboard strip to the size of the child's head and staple.
5. Staple crown to tagboard.

Dramatization
Now re-read the story and have the students respond in the appropriate ways.

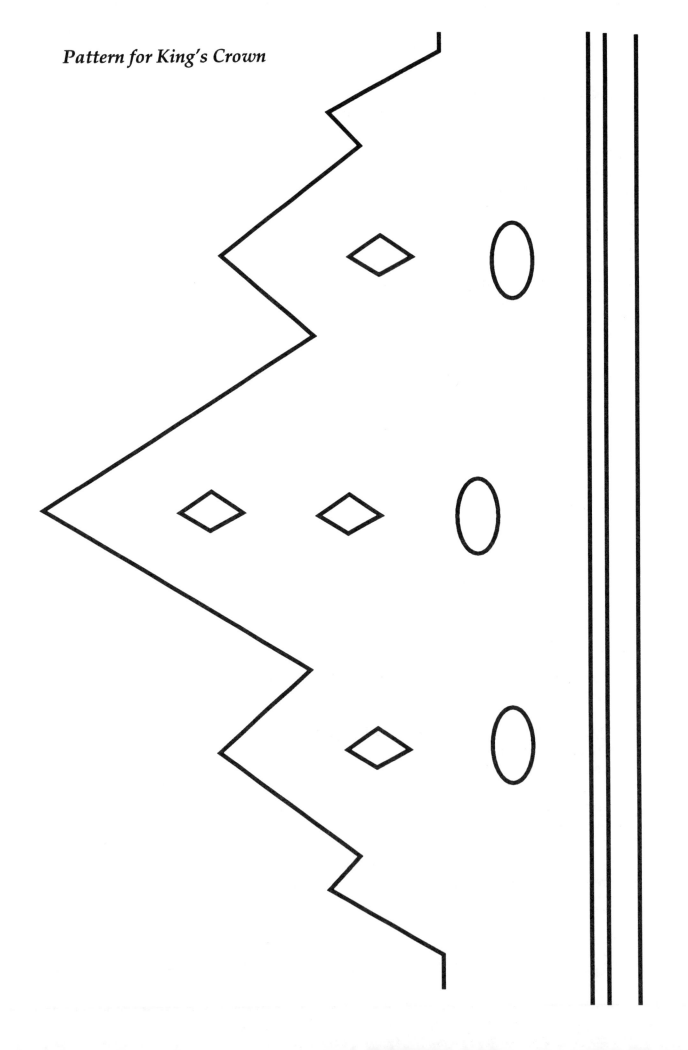

Pattern for King's Crown

The Call of Peter, Andrew, James, and John

Luke 5:2,4-11

Simon (later called Peter), his brother Andrew, and their partners, James and John, had been fishing all night in the Sea of Galilee. They had caught nothing. (^) Then Jesus came along and told them to try again. (^) And so they did. Soon the boats were so filled with fish that they were almost sinking. (^)

Jesus said to them, "Do not be afraid. Come and follow me. From now on you will be fishers of people."

Simon, Andrew, James, and John quickly pulled the boats up on the beach. (^) They then left everything and followed Jesus.

Movement and Dialogue Exercise

FISHERMEN—They had been fishing all night. What might their conversation be?
How would they be feeling?
What would their faces look like?
They were probably folding their nets on shore at this time. How would you show this?
Would their bodies be open or closed? Why?
Jesus tells them to try again. What might their first reaction be?
What would they say to Jesus in response?
What would their faces look like?
They try again. What action for fishing with a net?
What would they probably be saying to each other at first? When the nets are filled?
   How would they feel now?
What would their faces look like?
Jesus asks them to follow him.
Do you think they had to think very long about this? Why? How would they feel now?
They pulled in their boats. Actions?

JESUS—How would Jesus be standing and gesturing to the fishermen?
How would Jesus react when fishermen were reacting to all the fish they caught?
How would Jesus greet them when they return to shore?

Stage Setting

The first part has the fishermen on shore, probably folding their nets. After Jesus tells them to try again, they need to move to the other side of the stage for the fishing scene, then back again to the shore. It might be best to begin at the left and move to the right of the stage. No particular props are necessary, but small fish nets can be made as directed on page 11.

Characters

Narrator
Jesus
Peter
James
John
Andrew

Directions for the Fishing Net

You will need:
pattern for fishing net
a large sheet of paper about 35" x 35"

1. Begin by folding the paper in half and then in half again. (A and B)
2. Fold again, only this time on the diagonal. (C)
3. Cut into the sides about 1/2 inch apart, alternating sides. Do not cut all the way through! (D)
4. When ready to use, unfold net carefully.

Dramatization

Now re-read the story and have the children respond in the appropriate ways.

Pattern for Fishing Net

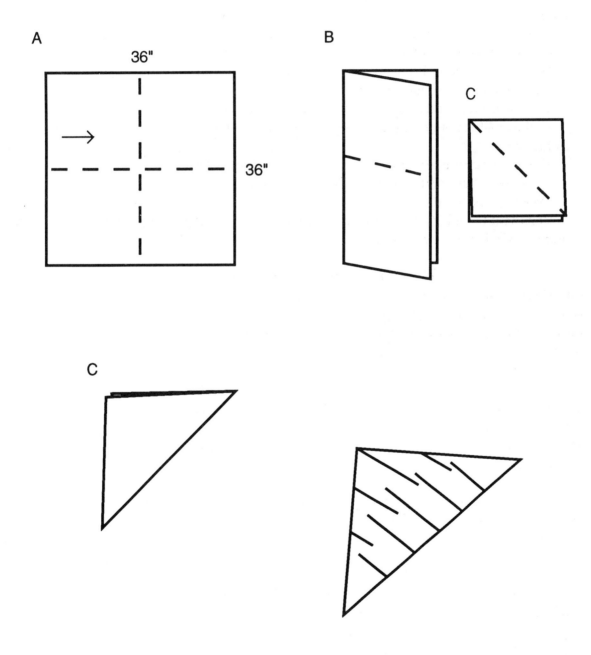

A

36"

36"

B

C

C

Bartimaeus, the Blind Man

Mark 10:46-52

One day Jesus was going through Jericho. As he was leaving the place with his disciples and a lot of other people, there was a blind beggar, Bartimaeus, sitting by the roadside.

When Bartimaeus heard that Jesus of Nazareth was going by, he began to call out, "Jesus, Son of David, have pity on me."

The people scolded him and told him to be quiet, (^) but he only shouted all the louder, "Son of David, have pity on me."

Jesus heard him and stopped. "Call him over," Jesus said.

So they called the blind man over saying, "Don't be afraid of him. Get up. He is calling you."

The blind man threw aside his cloak, jumped up and came to Jesus.

Jesus asked him, "What do you want me to do for you?"

"Master," the blind man said, "I want to see."

Jesus said to him, "Go. Your faith has saved you." At once he was able to see (^) and followed Jesus along the road.

Movement and Dialogue Exercise

BARTIMAEUS—What do you think it feels like to be blind?

What are some of the wonderful things a blind person cannot see?

Even though our eyes see, are there some ways in which we can still be "blind"?

Are we sometimes blind to a classmate who would like to join "our group"?

Do we pretend sometimes not to see how tired our parents are and let them do all the work?

Do we sometimes pretend not to see a job that has to be done?

Are we afraid to see some things?

The blind man in our story really wanted to see! How do you think he felt when the people tried to quiet him?

PEOPLE—Why did the people try to quiet him?

Have you ever tried to quiet someone? Why?

How did you try to quiet someone?

JESUS—How did Jesus feel about the man?

How do you think the people who had tried to quiet the blind man feel? Excited? A little afraid? Happy?

Jesus asks him right out what he wants and the blind man doesn't hesitate. He knows exactly what he wants. He wants to see! When someone helps you to see something that you have wanted to see, how do you feel?

Stage Setting

The movement in this story is from one side of the stage to the other. The crowd can be moving with Jesus and just a little ahead of him so that they hear the man before Jesus. The blind man is by himself, perhaps sitting on a little stool to represent a rock. The only costumes you may want are a cloak for the blind man and the usual red shawl for Jesus. A walking stick for the blind man would also be appropriate. If you wish more stage props, you might like to make a sign for Jericho and another sign pointing to Jerusalem, the place where Jesus was headed.

Characters

Narrator
Jesus
Bartimaeus
Crowd (one speaker)

Dramatization

Now re-read the story and have the students respond in the appropriate ways.

The Good Samaritan

Luke 10:25-37

One day a young man saw Jesus and wanted to test him. He asked Jesus a question. "Teacher, what do I have to do to live always in God's love?"

"What does it say in Scripture?" asked Jesus.

"You will love the Lord, your God, with all your heart, with all your soul, with all your strength, and with all your mind; and you will love your neighbor as you love yourself," replied the young man.

"That's right. Do that and you will live in God's love," Jesus said.

The young man felt foolish. He had just answered his own question. To cover up, the young man asked another question. "Who is my neighbor?" Then Jesus told this story.

One day a man was going on a trip from Jerusalem to Jericho. Robbers attacked him, beat him up, and stole his money. (^) They left him by the side of the road half dead. (^)

A little while later a priest walked by. He saw the man lying on the side of the road. (^) But he just walked right past him.

Soon another man, who thought of himself as a good person, came along. He saw the man lying on the side of the road. (^) But he, too, just walked right past him.

Then a Samaritan came along. A Samaritan was considered to be an enemy. (^) He saw how badly the man was hurt and felt sorry for him. He washed the man's wounds and bandaged them. (^) He lifted the man onto his donkey and took him to a nearby inn. (^)

The Samaritan stayed and cared for the man all day. (^) The next day the Samaritan gave money to the innkeeper. "Take care of this man until I come back. If you need to spend more money, I'll repay you when I return."

When the story was finished, Jesus looked at the young man. "Which of these three people acted like a neighbor to the man who was robbed?" asked Jesus.

"The one who was kind to him," replied the man.

"Then go and do the same," answered Jesus.

Note

The story about the Good Samaritan may be performed either by itself or in the context of the questions of the young man. There is more dialogue in this story so you may want to use cue cards. Also, you might want to teach the children the "freeze technique" (the players in the Samaritan story hold their final pose while Jesus and the young man finish off the story).

Have something for the robbers to hide behind and make a sign for the inn.

Movement and Dialogue Exercise

YOUNG MAN—The young man is something of a smart aleck.
How would his face look as he asks the questions?
What would his voice sound like?
When he realizes that he has answered his own question, what would his face look like?
How would it change when he then asks another question?

JESUS—How would Jesus respond to young man?
What tone of voice would Jesus use?

TRAVELER—How would he walk along before he gets robbed?
How would he be feeling?
When the man first sees the robbers, what would his face look like?
How would he try to defend himself?
How does he feel as he lies by the side of the road, beaten and half dead? Hurting?
In a lot of pain? Helpless? Afraid? Abandoned? Angry? Weak? Cheated? Foolish for
   having traveled without some protection?
Have you ever felt like this?

ROBBERS—Where would the robbers be hiding?
How would they be feeling?
What would their faces look like?
How would they come out of hiding?
What might they say as they are robbing and beating the man? As they run away?

OTHER TWO MEN—How would they pretend not to see the man?
Perhaps take one quick look at him and then look the other way?
How would they be feeling? Guilty? Scared? Disgusted? Superior?
How would they walk? Fast or slow?

SAMARITAN—How would his face look when he first saw the injured man?
What would the man say to the Samaritan?
Show me how he washed and bandaged the man.
How does he lift the man?

TRAVELER—How would the injured man feel now? How would he show it?

INNKEEPER—What would be his response to the Samaritan when he arrived with the
   injured man? When paid?

Stage Setting

On the left side of the stage area the dialogue between Jesus and the young man can take place. The actual story of the Good Samaritan can be done to the right. It can all be performed without any props but you might consider having another child play the donkey.

Costumes

If you wish to have a student play the part of the donkey, you can make a mask for him (her) found on pages 17-18.

Characters

Narrator
Jesus
Young man
Traveler
Robbers
Priest
Other men on road
Samaritan
Innkeeper
Optional: donkey

Directions for the Donkey Mask

You will need:
Mask pattern and ears for donkey
Brown construction paper or brown paper bags
Felt pen (brown or black) or crayon
Tagboard strip, 1 1/2" x 24"

1. Duplicate the mask and ears on brown construction paper or brown paper bag paper.
2. Cut out the mask and ears.
3. Cut out holes for eyes.
4. Shade the ears and draw in lines on face. Glue ears to mask.
5. Measure a tagboard strip to the size of the child's head and staple.
6. Staple the mask to the tagboard.

Dramatization

Now re-read the story and have the students respond in the appropriate ways.

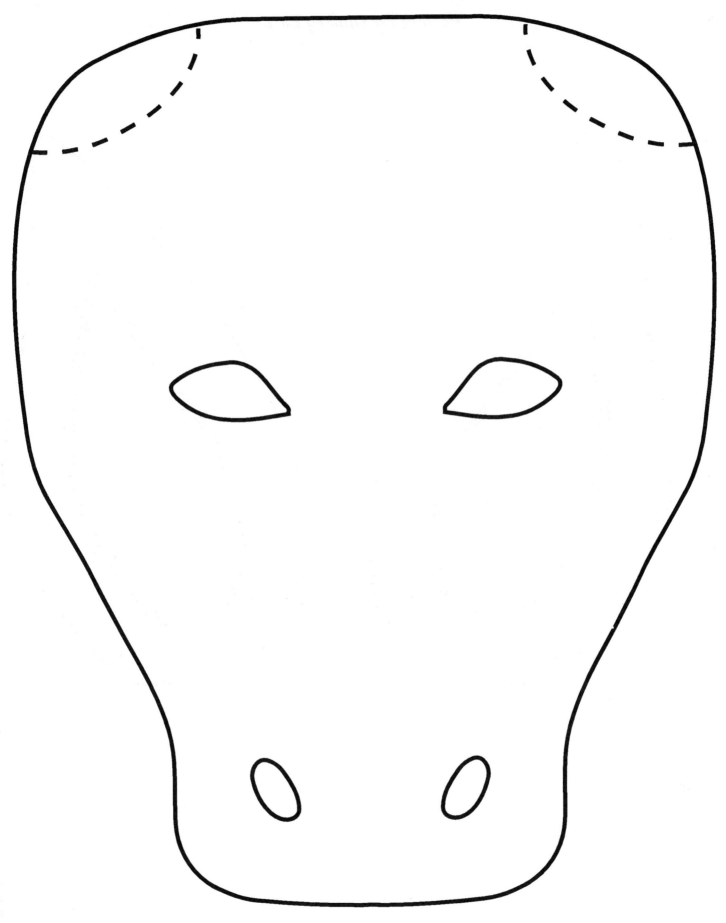

Pattern for Donkey Mask

Pattern for Donkey Ears

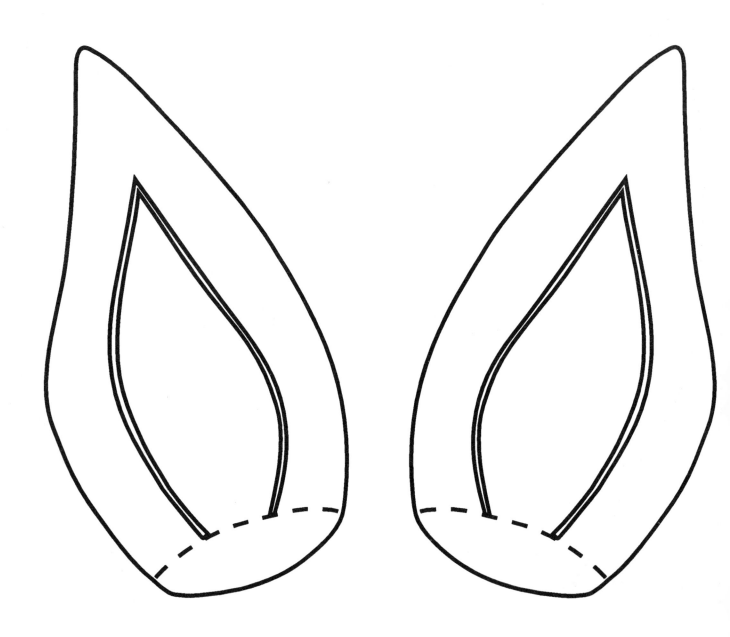

Zaccaheus

Luke 19:1-10

Zaccaheus was a short, little man who was very greedy. He had been appointed chief tax collector in the area. No one liked him because he collected extra taxes and kept them for himself.

One day Jesus was passing through Jericho. Zaccaheus heard the noise of the people (^) and wondered what was happening. He quickly put on his cloak and hurried out to see. Zaccaheus asked what was going on. (^) He was told that Jesus was going by. Zaccaheus wanted to see Jesus, but he was too short to see over the heads of all the people who had gathered. (^) He couldn't see around them either. (^) Then he saw a tree and had an idea. (^) Zaccaheus climbed the tree, and then he could see very well.

Soon Jesus was going by near the tree. The people were very excited. (^) When Jesus came close to where Zaccaheus was, he looked up and said, "Zaccaheus, come down. I want to stay at your house today."

Zaccaheus was so excited! (^) Jesus wanted to come to his house. He climbed down that tree so fast! And he told Jesus he was welcome to come with him. (^)

But the people became upset and began to mumble. (^) They knew Zaccaheus was a sinner. But Zaccaheus was so happy that Jesus had been kind to him that he changed completely. "Jesus, I am going to give half my things to the poor. And if I have stolen from anyone I will give back four times as much!"

Jesus was so happy! He said, "Today you have been saved. This is why I am here. To save the lost."

Movement and Dialogue Exercise

GREED—What is greed?

Why is it so evil?

How can we show greed? (Rub hands together...one hand held out flat while the other hand moves coins in the middle of the first hand.)

What would a greedy person's face look like?

Would the body be open or closed? Why?

DISGUST WITH ZACCAHEUS—How would the bodily actions of the people show their disgust? Their faces?

What would they say?

ZACCAHEUS HURRYING—Decide where Zaccaheus is to begin and where he is to go.

He is originally at home...he has to go out a door...How would he walk out the door?

What would his face look like as he goes out the door before he knows what all the noise is about?

ZACCHAEUS TRYING TO SEE OVER THE PEOPLE—Have you ever tried to see over taller people? What do you do?

What might you say to some of the people? In a crowd like this, do people listen much? What would be their responses to Zacchaeus?

ZACCHAEUS HAS AN IDEA—What would his face look like? Any body actions?

ZACCHAEUS CLIMBS A TREE—Discuss moving hands up the tree...one at a time...pulling oneself up onto a branch.

EXCITED PEOPLE—As Jesus came nearer, the people became excited. How would their faces look?

What would they be saying? How would their bodies show excitement?

JESUS—How would Jesus walk? What would his face look like?

He's talking to Zacchaeus up in the tree, so where would he be looking?

ZACCHAEUS CLIMBS DOWN THE TREE—What motions? His face? What would he say to Jesus?

UPSET PEOPLE—What would the faces of the people look like? What would they be saying?

ZACCHAEUS AND JESUS HAPPY—As Zacchaeus goes off with Jesus, would his body be open or closed? What would the faces of Jesus and Zacchaeus look like?

Stage Setting

Zacchaeus's home can be on the right side of the stage area with the crowd in the middle of the stage. Jesus will enter from the left. Behind the people, have a sturdy chair or similar item for Zacchaeus to climb up onto.

Characters

Narrator
Jesus
Zacchaeus
Crowd (one to speak to Zacchaeus)

Dramatization

Now re-read the story and have the students respond in the appropriate ways.

The Prodigal Son

Luke 15:11-24

One day Jesus told this story. A man had two sons. One day the younger son said to his father, "Father, I want to leave home and try living in the city. Give me my share of the family money so I can go." (^)

The father was sad! He wanted his son to stay at home with him. But the father did as his son asked. (^)

The son gathered together his things and went off to the city. He spent his money foolishly. (^) He was not responsible and only wanted to have fun. (^) Soon all of his money was gone. He had no food or clothes or work. He was very unhappy and lonely. (^) He finally found work on a farm, caring for pigs. The young man worked hard, but he wasn't paid very much. He was sometimes so hungry he wanted to eat the pig's food. (^) One day he sat down and thought of his father and the home he had left. "Even my father's servants have enough to eat. And here I am starving. I think I'll go back to my father and tell him how sorry I am. I guess I won't be able to be his son any more, but maybe I can work for him as one of the servants."

At home his father missed him very much. He watched for him every day hoping he would come back. The young man was still a long way down the road when his father saw him. The father ran as fast as he could to meet his son. (^) He hugged and kissed him. (^)

The son began to say he was sorry. "Father, I made a terrible mistake. I have sinned against God and against you. I no longer deserve to be your son."

"It's all right! I forgive you. The important thing is that you have come home. Servants! Quick! Bring my son some new clothes. Put a ring on his finger and shoes on his feet. Prepare a big feast. My son who was lost is now found." The father then took his son into the house.

When the older son returned from working in the fields all day, he heard the noise of a party. He asked, "What is going on?"

The father replied, "Oh, good news! Your brother has returned and we are having a celebration in his honor." But the older son was angry.

"All these years I have worked with you and have been faithful. But not once did you have a party for me! Your son who has wasted all your money on wine and women comes home and you throw him a party. I will not have any part of it." And he refused to come in.

The father replied, "All I have is yours. But now we must celebrate, for your brother has come back to life."

Movement and Dialogue Exercises
INTRODUCTION OF THE SONS—How might they both present themselves?

Would their faces be happy?
Their bodies, open or closed?

YOUNGER SON COMES TO FATHER—How would he approach his father?
How would the father feel when he hears the younger son's request?
How would his face show this?
What might he say to the son to try to talk him out of it?
Have your parents ever tried to talk you out of doing something?
How did you respond?
How would the son respond when the father said he would do it?

OFF TO THE CITY—How would the son walk as he went off to the city?
How would the city people welcome him?
How could we show him wasting his money?
One day he discovers he has no more money. How could we show this?
His friends disappear. He is alone. What would his face look like?
Would his body be open or closed?

CARING FOR THE PIGS—What would he say to the farmer to get work?
What would the farmer say to him?
How would he care for the pigs?
He talks aloud to himself about his hunger. What does he say?
He finally sits down and decides to go home. How does his body change? His face?

A WAITING FATHER—How does it feel to wait for something?
What are some things you have had to wait for? They might practice pacing the floor
    and looking down the road, hands over eyes to shade them.
How do the father's face and body change when he sees the son? (...he might not be-
    lieve it at first....)
How would the son be walking as he comes home? (If they say fast or slow, ask them
    why they think that. He is not sure how the father will receive him.)
As the son confesses his sins to the father, what would his voice sound like?
How would the father's voice sound? Angry? Excited? Happy?

SERVANTS—Although they have a very minor part, they should practice coming run-
    ning and then again going out to get the feast ready, maybe saying a few words of
    welcome to the son.

THE OLDER SON—He is coming in from working hard all day. How does he feel?
Would his body be open or closed?
At first he is confused. How would his face look?
Then, when he finds out what is going on, how does he feel? How does his face show
    this?
What might he say?
Does the father understand how the older son feels?
Is he willing to give in to him? Why not?

Do you think the older son ever joins the party? Why or why not?
Who do you think is right?
Do you, most of the time, feel like the younger or the older son?

Stage Setting

The scene changes several times in this story. However, very few props are needed. It might be fun to have a few masks for the pigs, just to add a little something to the production. See pages 24-25 for a possible mask. Having the "pigs" simply hold a paper cup in their mouth as a snoot also works.

If you have some cheap, glitzy clothes for the city friends to wear, it would be nice but not necessary. If you have a cloak for the father, fine.

Since the stage changes several times, you may want to make up the following large signs to help identify the setting; HOME, CITY, PIG FARM. These are not necessary, however, as young children have wonderful imaginations.

The opening scene is the home and can be played on the left part of the stage. The city can be to the right and the farm again to the left. When the son goes home, he can head off to the right and go around in a circle toward the original home on the left.

Characters

Narrator
Father
Younger son
Older son
Servants
Farmer
Pigs
City "friends"

Directions for the Pig Mask

You will need:
Pattern for pig mask and snoot
Light brown or light pink construction paper
A small piece of sponge
Pig mask and snoot
Piece of tagboard 1 1/2" x 24"

1. Run off mask and snoot on colored construction paper
2. Cut out mask and snoot. Cut holes for eyes.
3. Glue the snoot onto the mask with a small piece of sponge in between to set out the snoot a little.
4. Measure the tagboard to child's head and staple it onto pig mask.
5. Staple mask to tagboard.

Dramatization

Now re-read the story and have the students respond in the appropriate ways.

Pattern for Pig Mask

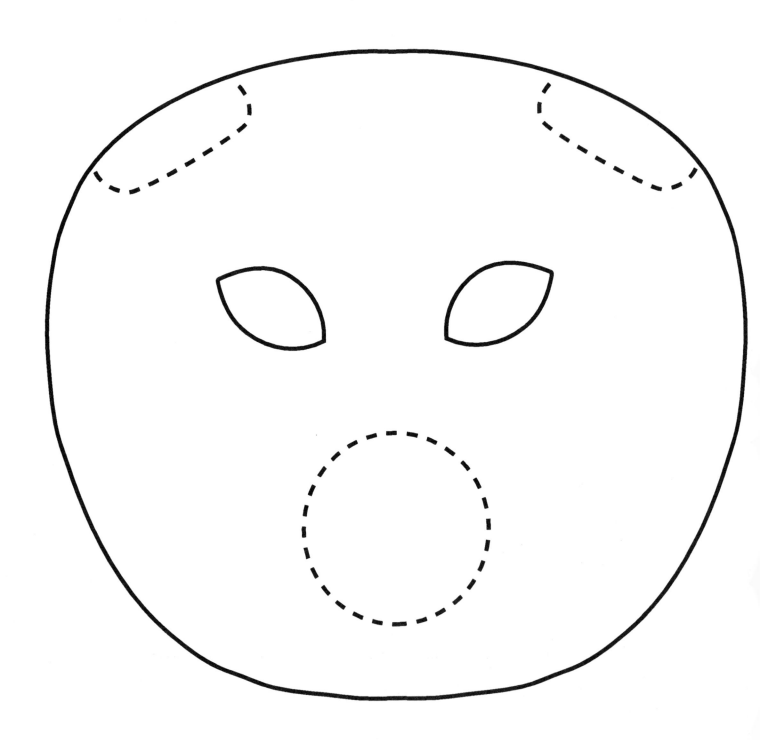

Pattern for Pig Snoot and Ears

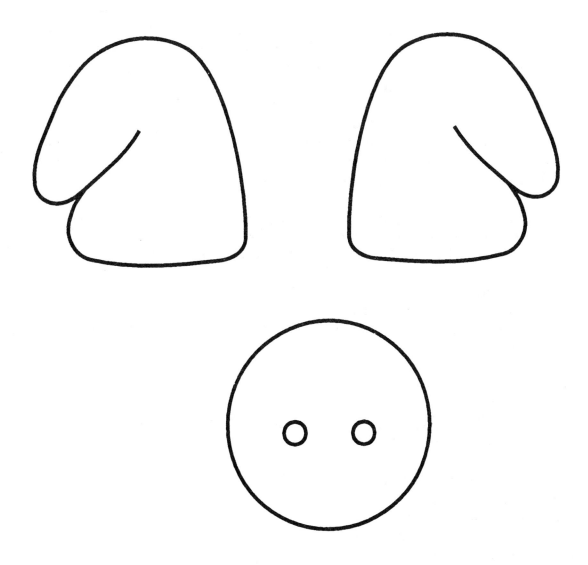

The Rich Man and Lazarus

Luke 16:19-31

Jesus told this story: There was a rich man who used to dress in only the best clothes and eat good food every day. (^) And just outside the door of his house sat a poor homeless man called Lazarus who was covered with sores. He was so hungry he longed to eat the crumbs that fell from the rich man's table. (^) Even dogs came and licked his sores. But soon the poor man died and was taken to where Abraham welcomed him. The rich man also died and was buried.

The rich man now had nothing, and he was in torment in Hades. He saw Abraham from far away and the poor man was with him. He cried out to Abraham, "Please, Father Abraham, have pity on me. Send Lazarus with a little water to cool my tongue, for I am in great agony in these flames."

But Abraham replied, "My son, remember when you had so much and Lazarus had nothing? Now he is comforted while you are in pain. But that is not all: between us and you is a huge gulf that no one can cross."

Then the rich man said, "Father, I beg you. Send Lazarus to my five brothers to warn them so they will change their ways before they die and not come to this place of torment."

Abraham replied, "Moses and the other prophets have already warned them."

The rich man said, "Oh, no, Father Abraham. Send someone from the dead. Then they will listen."

But Abraham replied, "If they would not listen to Moses and the prophets, they will not listen even if someone from the dead should come to tell them."

Movement and Dialogue Exercise

(Scene One) The Rich Man's House:

RICH MAN—How does he feel as he sits in his house, eating the rich food?
When he walks around, how would he walk?
What would his face look like?
Have you ever felt like a rich person?
How do you think he treated Lazarus as he walked past him each day?

LAZARUS—How does he feel, sitting and begging?
How would he walk around?
What would his face look like?
Have you ever felt like a poor person?
What would Lazarus say to the rich man as he passed by?

(Scene Two) Heaven and Hell

RICH MAN—How does the rich man feel now? Sorry? Angry? Surprised? He had some
  good in him.
How do we know this? (He wants to help his brothers.)

LAZARUS—How does Lazarus feel now?
Do you think he might pity the rich man?

ABRAHAM—We meet Abraham. What kind of person is he? What tone of voice would
  he use? (Kind but firm. A little sad that the rich man was lost.)
What gesture might he use when he talks about the gulf between them? (Large gesture
  of the arm to indicate an impossible distance.)

Note
Memorized Lines or Note Cards: This story has more given set lines than most of the
stories. However, if your students are good at improvising from what they know of the
story, let them do their own lines.

Stage Setting
(Scene One) In the first scene we recommend a few props to emphasize the differences.
A fancy goblet for the rich man along with some velvet or silk clothes. Lazarus could
have a few bandages around his hands, head, or leg, and perhaps a walking stick.
Abraham could be wearing a simple cloak or just a robe. The dog could be wearing the
mask as given on page 29.
  Left stage could have the rich man seated at the table eating, with a dog under the ta-
ble. Lazarus is sitting on the floor on right stage. When the narrator begins to talk about
Lazarus, the dog can go over to Lazarus and pretend to lick his wounds. At the same
time the rich man can exit to right stage simply ignoring Lazarus as he walks by him.

(Scene Two) Again have the rich man on left stage and Lazarus and Abraham on right
stage. Have them as far apart as space allows. Flames for the Hades scene can be made
ahead of time. Use red tissue paper or newspaper (use the ad section) and paint flames
on it. These can be taped to the side of a box and placed in front of where the rich man is
standing. Abraham and Lazarus can be seated together with Abraham's arm around
Lazarus.

Characters
Narrator
Lazarus
Abraham
Rich man
Dog (see page 29 for mask)

Directions for the Dog Mask

You will need:
Mask and ear patterns
Colored construction paper or brown bag paper
Colored pens (brown or black)
Strip of tagboard 1 1/4" x 24"

1. Run off mask and ears on construction or brown bag paper.
2. Cut out mask, ears, and holes for eyes.
3. Shade in parts of the mask with colored pens (brown or black).
4. Glue ears to front of mask at the top of head so that they flop down on front and side of dog's face.
5. Measure the tagboard strip to the child's head. Staple it to the mask.

Dramatization

Now re-read the story and have the students respond in the appropriate ways.

Pattern for Dog Mask

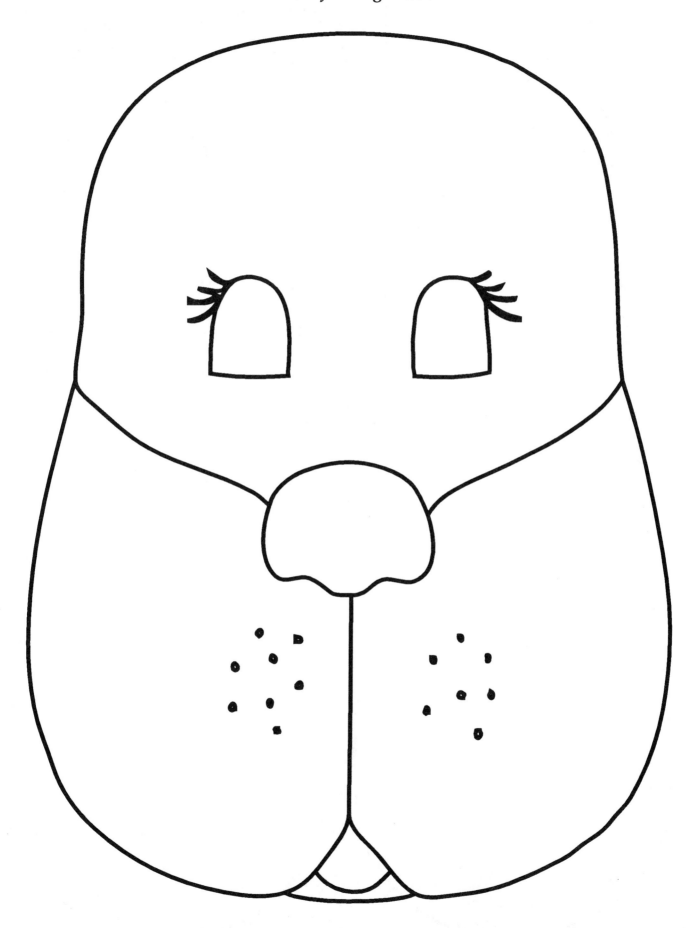

Pattern for Dog Ears

The Multiplication of the Loaves and Fishes

John 6:1-13

One day Jesus and his friends went up the mountain (^) and sat down. (^) Soon many people began to follow them. These people knew Jesus and wanted to be with him and to listen to what he had to say. (^)

Jesus talked to them all day, and by evening everyone was tired and hungry. Jesus asked the disciples about feeding the people. (^) Andrew told Jesus about a boy who had some food. "There is a boy who has five loaves of bread and two fish. He is willing to share them, but what is that with all these people?"

Jesus told the people to sit down. (^) There were over five thousand people who sat down on the grass.

Then the boy gave Jesus the bread and the fish. (^) Jesus thanked him. (^) Then he gave thanks to God for the food and told his friends to distribute it. (^) Everyone was fed and had as much to eat as they wanted. (^) There even was food left over! When the people realized what Jesus had done, they wanted to make him a king. (^) But Jesus went quietly away from there.

Movement and Dialogue Exercise

DISCIPLES—Going up the mountain they would probably use walking sticks. How would the climbing movement be?

How would they feel when they finally sat down?

What might they say as they were going up the mountain? When they sat down?

What might the disciples say when they saw the people who had followed? Why?

When Jesus asked the disciples about feeding five thousand people, what do you think their response would sound like?

Were the disciples tired, too?

Were they hungry?

What would Andrew's voice sound like as he told Jesus about the boy with the bread and fish?

BOY—How would the boy feel about giving the fish to Jesus? Proud? Happy?

Afraid he might not get any?

Do you think he was sad or joyful about his sharing?

How would Jesus receive the gift of the fish? Graciously? Just grab it?

PEOPLE—How do you think the people reacted when they were being given the food?

When they realized they could have as much as they wanted?

What would their faces look like?

31

Would they be less tired? Why?
What would they be saying to each other?
What would they say to Jesus?

JESUS—What does Jesus do? Why?
What would the people say when they realized there was food left over?
How would Jesus get away?

Note

The dialogue is simple enough that nothing needs to be memorized or put on note-cards. Andrew's direct quotation can be highlighted on narrator's copy so she or he knows not to read that line. Remind the narrator to allow plenty of time throughout the story for ad libbing.

Stage Setting

The climb up the mountain can be done until they get to the center of the stage area. The rest of the action takes place center stage.

You might want a basket for the bread and fish, plus a small stepping stool or two for Jesus and the disciples to sit on when they reach the mountain top.

Characters

Narrator
Jesus
Disciples
Crowd
Small boy

Dramatization

Now re-read the story and have the students respond in the appropriate ways.

The Daughter of Jairus

Mark 5:21-24, 35-43

Jesus was teaching by the sea when Jairus, a very important man from the synagogue, came up to him. Jairus fell at his feet and begged him to cure his daughter who was very sick. (^) Jesus got up to go with him. While they were on the way, some people from the sick girl's house came and told them that the man's daughter had died and that they should not bother Jesus any more. (^) Jesus ignored what they said (and said to Jairus), "Do not fear. Only believe." When they arrived at the man's house, there was a lot of noise with people crying and weeping loudly. (^) Jesus asked them, "Why are you weeping? The child is not dead, but only sleeping." And they all laughed at Jesus. (^)

So Jesus went inside along with the child's mother and father to where the child was. Jesus took her by the hand and said to her, "Little girl, I tell you to get up." And immediately the little girl got up and walked around. Jesus told them not to tell anyone about this (^) and to give the little girl something to eat.

Movement and Dialogue Exercise

JAIRUS—How do you think Jairus is feeling when he comes up to Jesus? Afraid of losing his daughter? Fear of being ridiculed? Desperate?

How would his face show these emotions? His body?

How do you think he feels when he is told that his child is dead? Despairing? Sad? Disbelieving?

How about when Jesus says, "Do not fear. Only believe"? A glimmer of hope? Confidence in Jesus? Confused?

How do you think Jairus feels when the mourners laugh at Jesus? Embarrassed? Afraid? Doubtful?

GIRL—How about the little girl? At first she is very ill and helpless. She is dependent on her parents to seek help for her. Perhaps she has a high fever and doesn't always know what is going on.

What might she be feeling? How do you feel when you are sick? How would your body show this?

How would she feel when Jesus tells her to get up because she is completely well? Surprised? Excited? Strong? Hungry?

How would she show this? What might she say?

PARENTS—How do you think Jairus and the girl's mother feel as she rises and walks? Overjoyed? Excited? Almost not believing what they are seeing?

JESUS—How do you think Jesus is feeling during all of this? When the messenger says the girl is dead? When the people laugh at him? When the girl gets up? How might he respond in his body to these things?

Stage Setting

The scene by the sea should be on one side of the stage area. The movement to the other side, where the girl is, is interrupted half way or center stage by the message that the child is dead. The raising of the child takes place on the other side of the stage.

Jesus should wear a red scarf. If you have a bed of some kind for the girl to lie on, it would be good. Otherwise, she could just be lying on a mat. Some kind of divider should be between the girl and the mourners, but it need not be elaborate.

Characters

Narrator
Jesus
Crowd
Jairus
People from the child's house
Mourners
Mother
Girl

Dramatization

Now re-read the story and have the students respond in the appropriate ways.

The Ten Virgins

Paraphrase of Matthew 25:1-13

The reign of God is like ten bridesmaids who took their lamps and went out to welcome the groom. (^) Now five of these bridesmaids were foolish, while the other five were wise. The foolish ones did not bring extra oil for their lamps, but the wise ones did. (^) The groom was delayed awhile. (^) As they waited for him they all began to feel tired and began to fall asleep. At about midnight someone shouted, "The groom is coming! The groom is here! Everyone go out to meet him!"

When they heard the shout the bridesmaids awoke. (^) They all looked at their lamps. They had all gone out while they were waiting. (^)

The wise ones had extra oil so they poured it into their lamps and lit them again. The foolish ones begged them for some of their oil. (^) But the wise ones said, "No. If we do give you some, we will not have enough for our lamps. You had better go to the store and buy yourselves some."

While they went off to buy their oil, the groom came. (^) The ones who had their lamps ready went in with him. Then the door was closed and locked. Later the other bridesmaids came back. They knocked on the door and begged to come in. "Master, master, open the door for us."

But he answered, "I do not know who you are. Go away." They were very sad. (^) The moral of this story is: Be ready all of the time since you do not know on what day or what hour you will need to be ready.

Movement and Dialogue Exercise

BRIDESMAIDS—The story tells us that these were bridesmaids. How do you think they were feeling?

What might they be saying to each other at the beginning of the story?

What would their faces look like? Show me that kind of face.

When you see someone carrying something that you do not consider necessary, what do you sometimes say to them? For example, if someone brings too many clothes for an overnight.

Do you think the foolish bridesmaids thought that the wise ones were foolish for carrying the extra jar of oil? Would they tell them so?

As time went on and the groom did not arrive, how would they begin to feel?

What would they say to each other?

Soon they began to fall asleep. Everyone show me how a person gradually falls asleep. Then the cry goes up and everyone comes awake! What would they say when they woke up?

Would there be confusion?

FOOLISH ONES—What would the foolish ones all of a sudden realize?

What would the wise ones be busy doing?

What would the foolish ones say? They would probably go from one wise one to another.

Does someone want to show me how the foolish ones would move from one to another, being very anxious?

What did the wise ones reply?

How would the foolish ones be feeling now?

WISE ONES—How would the wise ones feel?

The wise ones go with the groom in through the door. If the foolish ones are looking back as they go, and they see the door closing, how would they feel?

When the foolish ones get back and knock on the door, how do they feel?

What would their faces look like?

What would their bodies be like?

What would they be saying to each other as they turn away?

Stage Setting

Everything takes place in front of two doors. It would be good to have a large piece of cardboard to represent the doors, but it is not necessary. The patterns for the lamp and flame are found on page 38. As the lamps go out, the flame is just lowered into the lamp. Later the wise ones can pull them out again.

The movement is quite simple. The bridesmaids can enter from the left. As they become sleepy they can sit down in front of the door and fall asleep. When the foolish ones return to the village to buy more oil they can again exit to the left. The groom can enter from the right. This should all be reviewed with the children ahead of time, or let them decide when and where.

Costumes

No costumes are necessary. However, if you have long gowns for all the students it would be nice. The groom could have some kind of crown as if he were a prince or king. With regard to the number of bridesmaids, a couple can represent the five in each group if the class is small.

Characters

Narrator
Five foolish bridesmaids
Five wise bridesmaids
Messenger
Groom

Directions for Lamps and Flames

You will need:
Construction paper
Glue
Scissors
Tape or stapler

1. Trace pattern on construction paper.
2. Cut out pattern, including holes for handle.
3. Cut along dotted line.
4. Fold along lines marked A.
5. Glue flap B to bottom of other side of lamp.
6. Glue or staple at pairs of dots.
7. Insert flame at pointed end of lamp.

Dramatization
Now re-read the story and have the students respond in the appropriate ways.

Pattern for Lamp and Flame

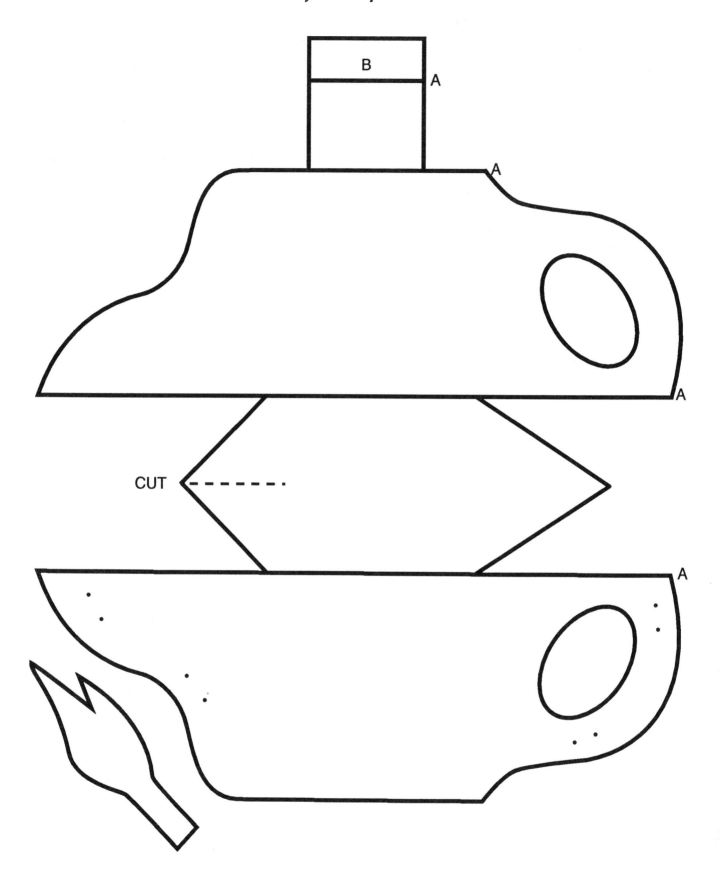

The Woman at the Well

Paraphrase of John 4:1-30

One day Jesus was on his way to Galilee with some of his disciples. (^) Jesus sent the disciples off to town to buy food. (^) Jesus was tired so he sat down at the well to rest. It was about noon and a Samaritan woman came to the well to draw water. Jesus said to her, "Would you please give me a drink?" The woman was really surprised that Jesus spoke to her because he was a Jew and because she was a woman. Most of the men at that time considered it improper to speak to a woman in public. The woman replied, "I'm surprised that you speak to me. You are a Jew and I am a Samaritan and a woman."

Jesus replied, "If you knew who I am you would know that I am a special gift to you from God. You would then ask me for water. And I would give you living water."

"Sir," she challenged him, "you do not have a bucket to get the water and the well is deep. How do you expect to get this living water?"

Jesus replied, "Anyone who drinks the water from this well will soon be thirsty again. But, if anyone drinks the water that I give, they will then have within them a fountain of water and will never become thirsty again."

The woman replied, "Sir, please give me this water so I don't have to come to this well every day to draw water."

Jesus replied, "Go call your husband and come back here."

She answered, "But I do not have a husband."

Jesus said, "You are right, But the truth is that you have had five husbands and the one you are living with now is not your husband."

The woman replied, "How did you know that? You must be a prophet!"

When the disciples returned they were very surprised to see Jesus talking to the woman, but they did not say anything. The woman left her water jar behind and went into the town and said to everyone she met, "I have met someone who told me everything that I have done. He must be the messiah!" And then they all came out to see Jesus. (^)

Movement and Dialogue Exercise

DISCIPLES—At the beginning of the story Jesus is walking with his disciples into this town. They have been walking all morning. How are they feeling?

What might they be talking about?

JESUS—Jesus then sends them into the town to buy food. How might he say this?

What do you think he would ask them to buy?

Is Jesus also tired?

He sits at the well, and along comes a woman. Do they greet each other? Why not?

But Jesus does speak to her. What does he say to her?

WOMAN—How will her face and her body respond to this request?

What does she reply?

Does Jesus get upset with her reply? What does he say?

Does she understand what he is saying?

How can you tell? (She thinks he is still talking about water we drink every day. Jesus is talking about "living water!")

After she replies, Jesus does not respond to her request, but instead asks her to bring someone to the well. Who is that? (her husband)

What does she reply? (But I do not have a husband.) How is she feeling at this point? How would her body and face show this? Why does she give this reply?

How does Jesus respond to her denial? (He tells her she is correct!)

And what does she respond? (How did you know that? You must be a prophet!)

So she now begins to recognize who he is.

DISCIPLES RETURN—Then the disciples return. They are probably talking to each other about what they bought. Then they see Jesus talking to the woman. What will be their reaction on their face and bodies?

Why don't they say anything?

The woman leaves without her jar. What is she feeling?

How will her face and body look?

What does she say to the townspeople?

TOWNSPEOPLE—What is their response?

What will they be saying as they go to see Jesus?

Note

This story is a little longer than most of the others in this book and has more dialogue. It will be important to go through the dialogue exercise carefully so children have the sequence of the dialogue in mind. Allow them a lot of leeway to improvise. They can also be prompted if necessary.

Stage Setting

A desk or cardboard box can serve for the well. It would be good to have a real bucket for the woman to have and leave behind. You will want to have a chair on which Jesus can sit. The well can be in center stage. Jesus and the disciples come from the left; the town is to the right. The woman also comes from the right at the beginning.

Characters

Narrator
Jesus
Disciples
Woman
Townspeople

Dramatization

Now re-read the story and have the students respond in the appropriate ways.

The Wedding at Cana

Paraphrase of John 2:1-11

One day there was a wedding in the town of Cana. Mary, the mother of Jesus, was there. Jesus and his disciples had also been invited to the celebration. (^) When the party was in full swing (^) they ran out of wine. Jesus' mother noticed this and felt sorry for the couple. She went to Jesus and said, "They have no wine." Jesus was a little surprised that she said this to him and he replied, "Why are you telling me this? My time has not yet come."

But Mary said to the servants, "Please do whatever Jesus tells you to do."

Now there were in the room six large jars which they used for their usual washings. Jesus said to the servants, "Fill these jars to the brim with water." The servants did as they had been instructed. (^) When the head waiter tasted it he was really surprised! This is what he said, (^) "What is this? I thought we were out of wine! And this is good wine!" He then went over to where the groom was and said to him, "This is such good wine! How come you have saved it until now? Most people serve the best wine first, and then only the poorer wine. But you have saved the best for now!"

This was the first miracle Jesus performed. When his disciples saw it they believed in him.

Movement and Dialogue Exercise

We know that Jesus prayed. He loved to talk to his heavenly Father. But Jesus also liked to have fun. And in this story we find him at a wedding.

DISCIPLES—How would Jesus and his disciples be feeling as they entered the house where the wedding is being held?
Would they be rowdy?
Would their faces and bodies show sadness?
What would they show?
At the beginning of our story Mary is at the wedding and Jesus and the disciples arrive.
What happened that almost ended the celebration?

COUPLE—How do you think the groom and bride felt when this happened?
How would their faces look then?

MARY—Mary notices the problem. How does she feel? She knows Jesus will also be concerned, so she goes to him.
What does she say to him? (They have no wine.)
How does Jesus respond? (Why are you telling me this? My time has not yet come.)
Mary does not say anything more. She just goes over to the servants, and tells them something. What does she tell them? (Please do whatever Jesus tells you.)

JESUS—What does Jesus tell them? (Fill these jars with water.)
How do you think the servants responded to this request?

SERVANTS—What might they say at first?
How is Mary feeling at this time? How is Jesus feeling?
How would they show these feelings in their faces? In their bodies?
The servants fill the jars. What does Jesus now tell them to do? (Now take some out of the jar and bring it to the head waiter.)
How might they respond? Remember, Jesus is asking them to take what they think is water to the head waiter!
What will the servants say to the head waiter when they bring him the new wine? (Not much, probably just ask him to taste it since he does not know where the wine came from.)
How does his face change when he tastes the wine?
What does he immediately do?
How do you think the groom responded?
What would the disciples say when they realized what happened?

Stage Setting

On the left stage can be the entrance to the wedding, as well as the place where the jars are sitting. Mary and her friends can be in center stage and the bride, groom, and their friends can be to the right stage. When beginning to tell the story, Mary and her friends and the groom, bride, and their friends can already be on stage. Jesus and his friends can then enter from the left and join the party. Everyone can more or less stay in these places until they have to move for the action. The servants can be moving around all of the time, doing their work. No props are necessary, but it would be nice to have some forms to represent the jars. The jars are large and need to be able to hold between twenty and thirty gallons. These can be cut out of cardboard or large pieces of newspaper and painted to look like large stone jars.

It might be nice to have a glass for the wine, but it is not necessary.

Characters

Narrator
Jesus
Disciples
Mary and friends
Groom
Bride
Friends
Servants
Head waiter

Dramatization

Now re-read the story and have the students respond in the appropriate ways.

Martha and Mary

Paraphrase of Luke 10:38-42

Narrator

One day as Jesus was traveling around he came to the village where Martha and Mary lived. They welcomed him to their home. (^) After Jesus had entered and made himself at home, Mary sat down at Jesus' feet and listened to everything Jesus had to say. (^) Martha, meanwhile, was busy trying to get the meal cooked for them. She became a little upset with Mary. (^) Finally she decided to say something to Jesus about it. "Jesus, excuse me, but don't you think that Mary should be helping me in the kitchen? Why don't you tell her to come and help me?"

But Jesus replied, "Martha, Martha, you are too anxious about things that are not really important. Mary has chosen the better part and I will not take it away from her."

Movement and Dialogue Exercise

JESUS—At the beginning of the story, Jesus has been traveling for a while. How do you think he is feeling?

How would his face show this?

How would his body show this?

When he first sees Mary and Martha, just seeing them may make him feel better. How would his face show this?

Show me on your face the change from tired to happy. What would they say to Jesus as they welcome him into their home?

MARY—After a while he is talking to Mary who is seated at his feet. What might he be telling her about? It might be good to decide on something definite; let the students decide. What would her face look like as she is listening?

MARTHA—Meanwhile, out in the kitchen, what does Martha feel?

How does her body show this?

How does her face show this?

What might she be saying to herself out loud? What does she finally decide to do?

What does she say to Jesus?

How would Mary be feeling at this time?

How would her face show it?

What does Jesus say to her?

What do you think happened after this? (Maybe they all decided to rest awhile and listen to Jesus, then *all* went out to the kitchen to prepare the meal, including Jesus.)

Stage Setting

This story is quite simple with not too much movement. Jesus can enter from left backstage. He can be seated on front left and the kitchen can be to the right. No props are necessary except for a chair for Jesus to sit down on.

Characters

Narrator
Jesus
Martha
Mary

Dramatization

Now re-read the story and have the students respond in the appropriate ways.

The Penitent Woman

Paraphrase of Luke 7:36-50

Narrator

Jesus was eating at the home of a pharisee named Simon. (^) A woman who lived in the town and had a reputation for being a big sinner, found out that Jesus was in town at Simon's house. She quickly went to see him. She brought with her a bottle of very expensive perfumed oil. When she came to Jesus she knelt down at his feet and began to weep. She wept so hard that her tears fell onto his feet. She wiped them with her hair, kissed his feet, and then poured the expensive perfume on them.

When Simon saw this, he said to himself. "This woman is a sinner! Everybody knows that. If Jesus were a prophet, he would know it, too!"

Jesus knew what Simon was thinking. So he said to Simon, "Simon, I want to ask you something."

Simon replied "Of course, what is it?"

Jesus said, "Let's say that there were two men. They owe a man some money. One man owes him five hundred dollars and the other one owes him fifty dollars. Now, neither one could pay him the money. So he says to both of them, 'Just forget about the money. You do not have to pay me back.' Now Simon, which of the two men would be the most grateful to him?"

Simon answered, "I guess the one who was forgiven the larger amount of money."

Jesus replied, "You are right." Then turning to the woman he said, "Do you see this woman? When I came to your home you did not give me water to wash my feet. She has washed my feet and dried them with her hair. You did not greet me with a kiss, but she has not stopped kissing my feet since she came here. You did not anoint my head with oil, but she has anointed my feet with precious oil. I tell you that is why her sins are forgiven: because she has much love. Little is forgiven to those who only love a little bit."

Then Jesus turned to the woman and said, (^) "Your sins are forgiven." The other guests present began to say among themselves, "Who is this that he can forgive sins?"

Meanwhile, Jesus said to the woman, "Your faith has saved you. Now go in peace."

Movement and Dialogue Exercise

When this story about Jesus begins, he is a guest at the house of a Pharisee. What was the Pharisee's name?

GUESTS—There were other guests too. They are seated around a table and are talking.

What do you think they are talking about? Let the students decide what they are talking about. You might want to have the students look in the Bible and see what has gone on just before this story. Decide on a definite topic for them to talk about.

WOMAN—Then, without any announcement or knocking on the door (remember, the houses are more or less open to the outside without the same kind of doors as we think of them) a woman who is a known sinner comes into the place where Jesus is sitting.
How will she be feeling?
How will her face show this?
How will her body show this? Will it be open or closed? Does she want to draw attention to herself?
What is she thinking?
What does she bring with her?
What does she do?

SIMON—Meanwhile, Simon is thinking. How can we have him speak his thoughts so that the audience knows what he is thinking?
What will his face look like as he has these thoughts? His body?
Jesus knows what he is thinking and says something. What does he say? (Simon, I want to ask you something.)
How does Simon respond?
How does his body change? His face?
Jesus responds by first of all telling him a little story. What is the story? Then Jesus asks him a question. What is the question? (Which of the two men would be the most grateful to him?)
Do you think that Simon knows what Jesus is getting at?
How is his body responding now? His face?
How does he answer Jesus? (I guess the one who was forgiven the larger amount of money.)

JESUS—Jesus tells him that he is correct. And then he turns to the woman. What has she been doing all this time?
What does Jesus tell Simon about her?
How do you think Simon is feeling now?
How might he be reacting with his body? His face?
After telling Simon how he felt about what he did not do and what the woman did, Jesus turns to the woman and tells her something. What does he say to her? (Your sins are forgiven!)
How do you think she responds with her face? With her body?

GUESTS—The other guests have been listening to all of this. What is their response?
How do their faces show what they are thinking and saying to each other?
Jesus continues to talk to the woman. What does he say? (Your faith has saved you. Now go in peace.)

Stage Setting

Everything takes place on center stage. Jesus is to the extreme left with other guests in the middle. Simon can be on the extreme right of where they are sitting. The woman enters from the left.

Costumes

No costumes are necessary, but nice if convenient. Jesus can wear the simple red cloth. If the student who plays the woman does not have long hair, she can wear a colored piece of material around her head to simulate hair, or the students can just pretend. She can carry a small jar for the perfume.

Characters

Narrator
Jesus
Penitent woman
Simon, the Pharisee
Other guests

Dramatization

Now re-read the story and have the students respond in the appropriate ways.

Of Related Interest...

Acting Out the Miracles and Parables

Sr. Mary Kathleen Glavich

52 playlets for the elementary grades that will enliven
and enrich religion classes.
ISBN: 0-89622-363-9, 142 pages, $12.95

Gospel Plays for Students

36 Scripts for Education and Worship
Sr. Mary Kathleen Glavich

Favorite and less familiar Gospel events scripted in
easy-to-understand language. For children of all ages.
ISBN: 0-89622-407-4, 112 pp, $12.95

Teaching the Bible with Puppets

Jeanne S. Fogle

Offers tips on puppet construction, staging, backdrops
and musical accompaniment, plus 17 sample scripts.
ISBN: 0-89622-405-8, 80 pp, $9.95

XXIII

*Available at religious
bookstores or from*

**TWENTY-THIRD
PUBLICATIONS**
P.O. Box 180
Mystic, CT 06355

1-800-321-0411